THE BEASTS' CHOIR

Also by Carmen Bernos de Gasztold
Translated by Rumer Godden

Prayers from the Ark

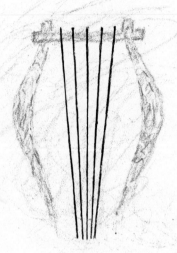

Decorated by

JEAN PRIMROSE

THE BEASTS' CHOIR

by

CARMEN BERNOS DE GASZTOLD

Translated from the French and with a Foreword by

RUMER GODDEN

MACMILLAN

LONDON · MELBOURNE · TORONTO

1967

First published in France under the title
Choral de Bêtes
1960 and 1965
© Éditions du Cloître
English Text: © 1965 by Rumer Godden
First published by Macmillan & Co. Ltd. 1967

MACMILLAN AND COMPANY LIMITED
Little Essex Street London WC2
also Bombay Madras Calcutta Melbourne

Printed by Charles Skipper & East Ltd   A member of the M^cCORQUODALE Group

CONTENTS

Carmen Bernos de Gasztold lives now in the *colombier*, the great dove-house converted to a guest-house, that belongs to the Benedictine Abbaye of St.-Louis-du-Temple in the rolling French countryside between Paris and Versailles. The Abbaye itself, with its farm buildings and its original château, is walled in its park but the dove-house tower stands apart, high and alone in the fields, open to such a wide sweep of land and sky that it seems the hub of the wheel of creation. From every window one can watch the landscape: clouds racing across the sky—it is a windy part of France—the blueness of still days; the larks winging up from the furrows; the return of the swallows. One can follow the cycle of the year, the tillage and manuring of the fields, the sowing and the crops; the seasons of wild flowers and trees; and, as well, the minuscule shy active life of country creatures. Indeed that tower seems a symbol of Carmen de Gasztold's talent in these poems of *The Beasts' Choir*, in which each creature is itself yet a part of the large world. 'Anyone could write such poems,' said one critic when she first showed them to him. Perhaps the simplest answer to such obtuseness is that no one else but Carmen de Gasztold has ever done it.

Her first book, *Prayers from the Ark*, brought her renown; the initial American printing was sold out in five days; since then there has been printing after printing: translations into German,

Dutch, Spanish, Italian, Finnish; a recording published by Folkways and exquisitely spoken in English and French by Marion Seldes, while a setting to music is on the way. There has been, in fact, a best-selling success, but *The Beasts' Choir* has not been written as a sequel. I found both books together some four years ago when they were in pamphlet form in French, published by the Éditions du Cloître, the Abbaye's private press and in which they had had something of a 'hidden life'. I resolved then that this second book, too, must be translated.

Most of these new poems are not prayers, in the sense that a prayer is a plea: each animal, bird, fish, reptile, or insect voice makes, as it were, a statement of its situation, its circumstances—what, perhaps, we humans would call its problem. Some of the voices are assertive, lacking the humility that made the Prayers so poignant, but each is exactly true.

I have learned to trust Carmen de Gasztold. Once or twice I questioned a line: 'A toad does not *flûte* as in the French; it croaks.' 'No,' said Carmen, 'it sings', and described for me the toads' night song. Why, I asked myself, does she say of the seagull that it is a 'bird of unending bitterness' (*l'amertume sans fond*)? On the day I asked that, I found in the London *Times* an account of an old sailor's sea lore in which he said that gulls were possessed of the souls of dead sailormen from Liverpool. 'Listen to their cry, "sca-a-ouse".' (Scouse, as every sailor knows, means a Liverpudlian.) Those with black heads, he believed, were once bosuns, black symbolising the wickedness of their hearts! The English poet Charlotte Mew, too, speaks of Westminster gulls that are old sea-captains' souls. Again and again Carmen de Gasztold shows that in a few lines she can catch the essence, the *être*, of a creature and without sentimentality—indeed, she

12

discovers that some have most dislikeable traits; but why should we take it for granted that beasts are born with 'nice' characters? Kindness, the virtue in humanity extolled nowadays more than any other, is completely lacking in animals; yet their faults—if these can be called faults—are redeemed by innocence, a quality human grown-ups have almost always lost.

Unlike the Prayers, humans seldom come into *The Beasts' Choir*; most of the poems are a direct communication between the beast, large or small, and its Creator, and the link is as powerful with the flea as with the whale—though the flea, being a flea, is less respectful. Carmen de Gasztold, as I said in the Preface to *Prayers from the Ark*, lives in an atmosphere of prayer, more importantly of belief, and none of her creatures questions for a moment that it has a creator, but her poems have not been influenced by the Abbaye; she is too independent to be influenced by anyone, and though the poems are Catholic in origin they are catholic also in the sense that they are for everyone, no matter of what creed.

The translation was difficult. The title itself brought a puzzle: the French is *Choral de Bêtes*, but in English 'choral' or 'chorale' is purely musical and also sounds a little affected, whereas 'choir: a company of singers', though not the exact translation, seems to fit the book. Then *bêtes*: to some ears 'beasts' carries only its meaning of brutishness, coarseness; yet to those who know of the Queen's Beasts (here in England), or of Helen Waddell's beautiful book *Beasts and Saints*, the word has its first meaning, as given in the *Oxford Dictionary*, of 'a living being' which covers animals, birds, fishes, insects, and reptiles. They all have a voice here.

As always, the smaller the poem, the greater the difficulty of translating because every word becomes more important, and

13

French to English is perhaps most difficult of all; for instance, in what one might dismiss as a trivial matter, the definite article, the French has genders, giving the play on *le*, *la*, *les*, whereas in English there is only 'the' that is apt to recur again and again, weighing down a short poem by its thick 'th'. At times too, I had to avoid the negative interrogative which in the English use of the verb 'to be' can sound stilted. There are different subtleties of meaning, such as the word *flûte* used of the toad: in French it gives the feeling of the range of the instrument's notes while in English it immediately suggests the treble—and though the toad sings, it certainly does not sing treble. Again, the rhythms of the two languages are very different: a French gnat has *la danse de St. Guy* with its five short dancing syllables, but an English gnat has to suffer from St. Vitus's dance which sounds slurred and hissing; for the vocation of the French beaver, the poet uses the word *édifier* with its double implication of spiritual raising as well as physical: 'to build' is the nearest one can get. These double meanings, the play on words and sounds, run all through the poems; in 'The Flea' the word *puce* in French means not only a flea but a colour so that the poet was able to get the double play of *ma robe puce*. Translated, the line becomes meaningless, so that we cut it; and there is always the untranslatable phrase such as *arrière pensée* in 'The Centipede'. *Arrière pensée* has a suggestion of rancour and darkness, and 'afterthought' or 'second thought' come nowhere near; but 'reticences' expresses thoughts withheld and silences not altogether normal, a little uncanny.

All through the book I was given considerable freedom to transpose lines or 'turn' them so as to get, not only what seemed to me the best effect, but closest to the poet's thought.

For us both, it was a time of comradeship; Carmen de Gasztold has no English, but letters and poems, both English and French, went backwards and forwards between the tower in France and my study in England, and when I came to the Abbaye itself we worked in one of the parlours. Were rooms ever better named? The amount of 'parlering' (if one can coin such a word) that goes on in them, is extraordinary, and the personality of the nuns is such that the grille* seems to disappear; but to work is one thing, to succeed is another and, as with the *Prayers from the Ark*, I am aware that I have not captured the poems in their original worth. There is an elusiveness, too, about these voices that led the poet to write the fleeting small poem at the end of this book. Yet, elusive or not, I feel Carmen de Gasztold has been able to find for each beast its authentic voice and this in a refreshing, matter-of-fact way; yet each large or infinitesimal, favoured or ill-favoured, bold or timid creature wafts up, as in the Prayers, an unexpected grain of incense that consecrates its wild or tame work-a-day self.

RUMER GODDEN

*The nuns are enclosed.

THE BEASTS' CHOIR

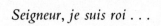

Seigneur, je suis roi . . .

THE LION

Lord,
I am King.
That is the law.
You know what it means
to wear a nimbus.
Some people think
they can rule by love.
How naïve!
I know how to govern
Your creatures:
strength
is all they respect.
Let us say
that fear is wholesome,
besides I delight
in making the whole plain tremble
with one roar.
Yet, far be it from me
to do anything paltry
or low;
I know the cost of a noble heart.
That is why,
Lord,
I so love Your glory,
and strive to attain it.

                    Amen.

. . . je suis Votre agneau
dans ma douceur de laine.

THE LAMB

A spindle on four legs
leaving tufts of white in the thickets,
I am Your lamb,
Lord,
in my soft wool.
My bleating
sends its puny note
into the ewe's heart,
my fleece
throws its curly shadow
on the cropped grass.
Look, Lord,
how my joy must leap!
Yet my need of my mother
never sleeps in me.
Let me run to her
with my wavering steps
and draw some of her tenderness.
Oh,
don't let it happen,
Lord,
that one sad day
I will miss her.

                              Amen.

A petits pas innombrables
je traverse la vie . . .

THE CENTIPEDE

With innumerable little footsteps
I go through life
but, Lord,
I can never
get to the end of myself!
It's a queer sensation
to be a multitude
that follows itself
in Indian file!
True,
it's the first step that counts
or, rather,
the first foot.
All that matters
is to be in step
with one's self.
I only ask,
Lord,
to jog along
one in spirit
without troublesome
reticences.

                          Amen.

Qui vit, qui vit, qui vit,
Seigneur,
si ce n'est moi?

THE SWALLOW

Who is quick, quick, quick,
and lives Lord,
if not I?
Small black arrow
of Your blue sky.
I stun the wind
by the swift ease
of my flight
but, under the eaves of the roof,
in their cosy clay home
my nestlings are hungry.
Quick, quick, quick,
in the hunt for their food,
I dart
from the top to the bottom
of heaven
with a whistle of joy,
then my beak opens
to snap up some inalert fly.
Lord,
a day will come,
a chill gold day
when my babes will take wing
on their own affairs.
Oh! On that day,
when there will be nothing more to bring,
console me
with the call of countries far away.

                    Amen.

Moi,
je me traîne, je me traîne, je me traîne . . .

THE SNAIL

Lord,
You try for a little while
to walk on one foot
carrying Your whole heaven on Your back.
As for me,
I drag, drag, drag on,
trailed by my iridescent track,
and swaying this hollow mountain,
my small house;
but where is there a coilaway
from gardeners and hens?
You must admit, Lord,
You have made my life hard.
So many enemies!
And just to bring home
the smear of my helplessness,
these two eyes on the tips of my horns,
are two timid periscopes.
Lord, You know
that someone who drags along complains.
Don't be offended
by this misanthropic heart
but, to lighten its burden,
send a paradise of lettuces—for one—
and the warmth of a thunder-shower.

                          Amen.

Rapide,
légère,
le cœur enlacé
de crainte sauvage . . .

THE GAZELLE

Fleet,
light,
my heart stifled
with wild fear,
always ready to leap
away with the wind,
at the least noise,
the least cry,
I bless You
Lord,
because for me
You have set no bounds
to Your space;
and if I fly,
an arrow
on my slender legs,
my little hooves
barely skimming the ground,
it is not that I scorn
the peace of Your pools,
but so, Lord,
that my life
might be a race
run straight
to the haven of Your love.

                              Amen.

. . . j'ai l'air
  d'une étoile de sang.

THE STARFISH

Lord,
Your deep has closed over me.
Am I
some small Lucifer
fallen from heaven
and left
to be tormented by the waves?
Look, Lord,
I seem
a star of blood.
I try to remember
my lost royalty
but in vain.
Creeping over the sand,
I spread my star-points wide
and dream, dream, dream. . . .
Lord,
an angel
could root me up
from the bottom of the sea
and set me back
in Your sky.
Oh! One day
could that be?

                    Amen.

. . . la joyeuse ardeur de mes ailes
pleines de petits yeux noirs!

THE LADYBIRD

Dear God,
I belong to Our Lady, Your Mother.
That isn't hard to believe,
it's written in my name.
Oh! May my midget
thanksgiving,
the small circles of my flight
across the meadow
gladden Her heart.
How I love each blade of Your grass!
I love to land there,
resting the happy whirr of my wings—
dotted with small black eyes.
Thank You for having made me
so that no one is afraid of me;
a little toy,
a penny toy,
a mite of comfort and laughter.

Amen.

33

Oui, Seigneur, je pique!

THE HEDGEHOG

Yes, Lord, I prick!
Life is not easy
—but You know that—
and I have too much on my shoulders!
I speak of my prickles
but thank You for them.
You at least
have understood me,
that is why You made me
such a pin ball.
How else can I defend myself?
When people see me,
my anxious nose
searching for the fat slugs
that devastate the garden,
why can't they leave me alone?
Ah! But when I think proper,
I can roll myself up
into my hermit life.

                    Amen.

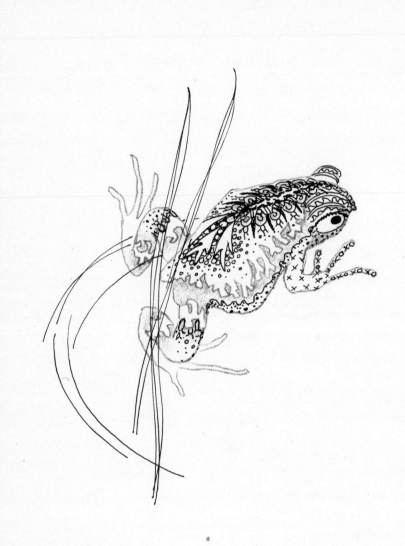

Solitaire et laid . . .

THE TOAD

Lonely and ugly—
who hasn't a horror
of me, Lord?
Yet my song trills
of an unmalicious heart.
In the night
that hides me,
I dedicate
the melancholy chant
of my unwholesomeness
to You, Lord.
Of Your mercy
graciously accept it,
and at last I shall learn
to bear my odium
with love.

                  Amen.

Ah! Quel souci!
Tous ces poussins . . .

THE MOTHER HEN

Oh! What a worrit!
All these chicks
to cherish and protect—
can't shut an eye
even for a moment!
That one strays too far,
those two big ones quarrel
and this tiny one isn't strong.
I should like to keep them always under my wings,
but they must learn how to live.
That dreadful cat!
Never trust a cat!
And all these feet
tramping round my brood.
Beware! Hen pecks!
I'm going to lose my temper!
Lord,
my heart is so choked
with loving care,
how can I say

                    amen?

*. . . l'orgueil a du bon
contre la soif, les mirages
et le vent de sable!*

THE CAMEL

Lord,
do not be displeased.
There *is* something to be said for pride
against thirst, mirages
and sandstorms;
and I must say
that, to face and rise above
these arid desert dramas,

two humps
are not too many,
nor an arrogant lip.
Some people criticise
my four flat feet,
the base of my pile of joints,
but what should I do
with high heels
crossing so much country,
such shifting dreams,
while upholding my dignity?
My heart wrung
by the cries of jackals and hyenas,
by the burning silence,
the magnitude of Your cold stars,
I give You thanks, Lord,
for this my realm,
wide as my longings
and the passage of my steps.
Carrying my royalty
in the aristocratic curve of my neck
from oasis to oasis,
one day shall I find again
the caravan of the magi?
And the gates of Your paradise?

                              Amen.

Je creuse, je creuse . . .

42

THE MOLE

I dig and dig,
looking
for life itself.
You have chosen darkness
for me, Lord.
and my tunnel
lengthens
in cavernous night.
Here and there,
a tiny hillock
shows above ground,
the rest
is buried
in the deep dark.
A hidden life,
Lord,
but not a poor one—
my velvet coat shows that.
In shadowy gloom
one can walk without presumption
and be perfectly safe—
but the sun
can turn one's head;
Lord, keep me from the vanities of the world,
and guide the strivings
of my little paws
so that they reach
some secret Paradise.

                              Amen.

. . . une *flèche ardente*
sur un mur de soleil.

THE LIZARD

Lord,
who has inlaid
the triangular throb
of my head
with these thirsting eyes,
and inlaid me
with a flicker quick heart,
please put me
a swift arrow
on a sun-baked wall:
a wall full of cracks,
of mossy havens,
quiet caves of shadow
and hiding places:
a wall alight with joy
and life . . .
let me drink at the fire of Your sky,
until a slit
in the walls of Your paradise
drinks me in, as a trickle of water
dries and is gone.

                    Amen.

sans doute
une plaisanterie divine . . .

THE WHALE

What could hold me,
Lord,
except Your ocean?
My inordinate size
must obviously be
a divine joke,
but am I
perhaps
rather ridiculous,
like a blown-up blubber toy?
I am a peaceful leviathan,
on a strict diet,
a waterspout
on my nose.
My sole problem
is to choose between water and air;
but,
hunted for my mollifying oil,
I dread the whalers
who mercilessly chase me
with their iron harpoons.
I never asked
for such yards of flesh,
and where can I hide
from the lust of men?
Lord,
if only some fortunate plunge
would let me come up into
Your eternal peace.

                              Amen.

. . . Votre soleil
me donne
la danse de St. Guy . . .

THE GNAT

Oh Lord,
Your sun
gives me
St. Vitus's dance,
I,
and all my clan.
We trace our strange ballet
in the sunlight.
Yes, we, though so little,
must manifest
our joy,
and dance, dance, dance.
Oh, let our tiny black constellation
take its place, one day,
glorified
as stars.

                              Amen.

49

. . .je suis
    quelque peu bavard . . .

THE PARROT

id You say something
Lord?
Oh! I thought
You were speaking to me.
You are silent?
Are You afraid
I shall tell
Your secrets?

It's true
I'm a little talkative
but, at times,
that is useful:
heads are thick,
slow to understand,
and have to be told things
again and again.
If You need me,
I am Your servant,
one who never grows tired
repeating the same word
again and again,
which has its power;
I may grow tedious
but people listen
in spite of themselves;
and what is repeated,
stays in the memory.
When may I serve
Your infinite wisdom?
Think of it, Lord.

                    Amen.

. . . au centre
de mon grand filet
de soie,
fragile et fort . . .

THE SPIDER

I thank You,
dear God,
for the arches
of my long legs—
a spinner's legs.
In the middle
of my wide silken net,
fragile and strong
in the shifting wind,
I wait for my meat and drink
and thank You,
dear God.
Between branches in the garden
I fish for frost and dew.
In the corners of dead rooms,
in dark attics,
I fish for sombreness,
lonely relinquishment,
and I thank You,
dear God.
In the nimble silence
of my life,
on the thread of my airy dreams,
in the geometric tracery of my thoughts,
I thank You,
for ever, dear God.

                              Amen.

Vous m'avez faite
tenace à ce qui m'attire . . .

THE FLY

Lord,
shall I always go in black
for this life?
Fugitive from its tumult
on my transparent wings,
humming my prayers
and pausing weightless
on my thin legs,
I,
whom the world finds such a burden?
You have made me
stick to what lures me.
Yet, if I am caught
clinging there,
don't let me die
like the poor useless
thing that I am.

                              Amen.

55

. . . mon plumage
est semé d'yeux
qui s'admirent.

THE PEACOCK

A royal train,
Lord,
more scintillating
than jewelled enamel.
Look,
now I spread it in a wheel.
I must say I derive
some satisfaction
from my good looks.
My feathers
are sown with eyes
admiring themselves.
True,
my discordant cry
shames me a little—
and it is humiliating
to make me remember
my meagre heart.
Your world is badly made,
if I may say so:
the nightingale's voice
in me
would be properly attired—
and soothe my soul.
Lord,
let a day come,
a heavenly day,
when my inner and outer selves
will be reconciled
in perfect harmony.

                    Amen.

Humide et glauque
dans ma petite maison
de nacre . . .

THE OYSTER

Moist, glaucous,
in my mother-of-pearl house,
its door tightly shut
against intruders,
I drink in a dream from the sea.
Oh, let an iridescent pearl—
a milky dawn,
a faerie sheen—
find its tints in the heart of my life.
Then if, slowly,
day by day,
this mysterious seed
grows more perfect,
for my joy
and Your glory,
Lord,
nothing else will matter.
If it must be, I shall die
to let it reach its fullest splendour,
shining—only for You,
Lord—
at the bottom of the sea.

                              Amen.

Je suis l'oiseau
de l'amertume sans fond,
blanc et gris
comme le sel. . . .

A hole in the cliffs
is my nest but the sea calls me,
and I cradle my dreams
in the hollows of the waves.
The roll of Your ocean
is with me in the sky,
where I swing
on one wing, then the other,
and plummet
like a stone
on the living flash
of a fish.
Lord,
does my poignant cry
echo the endless travail
that beats on Your shore?
I am the bird
like salt,
grey and white,
a bitter tang
that does not fade;
and the ships,
outward bound
watch me out of sight,
a little handkerchief
waving good-bye.
In the restlessness of my kingdom,
Lord,
let the storm spare me.

                    Amen.

Seigneur,
ayez pitié
de mon cœur d'ours.

THE BEAR

To have my name
among the stars,
then to think
I may end as a bedside rug!
Oh, Lord,
this thought makes me
terribly gruff.
Large-pawed, clumsy—
no teddy bear—
I am more shrewd
than people think,
and I know
all about climbing trees!
If I could find
a honeycomb,
my carnivorous soul
would not scorn its sweetness.
Sweetness!
There are men
who tame me,
and make me dance
to their piping;
or put me in a cage,
I, who was born to be free
like all self-respecting beasts.
Lord, have pity
on my bearish heart.
See to it
I meet no hunters.

Amen.

Je saute, je pique,
je saute, je pique!

THE FLEA

I jump.   I bite.
I jump.   I bite.
How it amuses me,
Lord!
How ingenious
to have made me so small,
with this springboard leap!
I jump.   I bite.
I jump.   I bite.
A royal game.
I own I put
a spice of malice in it,
and I have more power
to upset the world
than the elephant.
When I think of that
I could die of laughing.
I jump.   I bite.
I jump.   I bite.
Lord,
will You let me
into Your paradise
and not be afraid
that I shall turn it upside down?
I dare not say

                              amen.

. . . je ne demande
  qu'à bâtir
  Votre paradise.

THE BEAVER

To build,
Lord,
that is a vocation!
I speak of my passion,
architecture.
Of course
one should build on a rock,
but what fillip is there
in doing anything easy?

Tell me
to build a safe and steady house
on the moving stream
of a river—
moving as life does, swiftly—
what an adventure!
My element
is to struggle—
it is water that allures—
with patience and ingenuity
one can do anything.
But I am one
who loves to swim against the current,
to build
something lasting
—and all my own work—
at the very core of life.
Oh yes, Lord,
if You would give me
some of Your living water,
I would build
Your paradise for You.

Amen.

Little song
where is your heart?
In passing
you throw me a quick word
and escape on the wind.
I wish I could catch you
by the tip of a wing,
to get to know you,
laugh and cry with you.
Little song,
nobody's, anybody's,
you take your own fanciful way,
and drop your words
one by one
into my ear
and are gone.
Little song,
where is your heart?